My Illusion

Allina Raja

BookLeaf Publishing

India | USA | UK

Presentation by *BookLeaf Publishing*

Web: www.bookleafpub.com

E-mail: info@bookleafpub.com

ISBN:

First edition 2022

DEDICATION

My Father helped me get through the darkest days of my life.

Thankyou for saving me.

PREFACE

You made me unrecognisable
to myself
I look in the mirror
and think
who is she

Butterflies

At the sight of his eyes,
I forgot
how to breathe.
God knows how he must
look in the mirror.

Stubborn Heart

I know,
you won't return.

Yet the heart
is busy waiting.

I know
the moment this heart,
forgets about you,
It will be
my last day.

I want to go home

3

These days
I'm an empty bottle,
longing to return
to a home,
that never was.

It seems
I have become,
a foreigner,
In my own
reality

Lost

If you were a dream,
it would have been,
okay.

But
oh, cruel universe
played a game.

Made you
my reality,
and snatched you
away.

Now I sit alone
in a crowd.
Waiting for you.
I am lost
without you.

A Wish

Oh you
my world,
It's better this way,
that you stay
a lifelong wish.

If one receives the world,
one wouldn't think of it
as the world,
anymore.

Tears

Those who know
the pain
of losing someone,

know,

These are not tears of sadness.
These are not tears of joy.
They are just tears,
just let them fall.

You

Of course I don't get tired
of looking
at you,
all day.

Perhaps,
your picture
gets tired
of me,
staring.

Mine

Your eyes,
show a story.
A story that was supposed to be
mine.

Your mouth,
tells a story.
A story that was supposed to be
mine.

Your hands,
write a story.
A story that was supposed to be
mine.

You were supposed to be
mine.

My Own Reality

Whether you
become mine,
or not,
it's in fates hands.

I stay at peace
imagining,
you're only mine.

Neverending Nights

The days
go by,
It's the nights,
that drive me crazy.

When it passes over you,
you will know.

Ripples

I was once content,
admiring my reflection
in the water.
Just as someone came
and threw a stone.

I lost myself
ever since.

Again

Today, again
the heart made a wish.

Today, again
I comforted the heart.

Regret

What will people say?

This one sentence,
buried millions of dreams.

Disappeared

Where are you?

You said
you'd check up on me,
every night.

Have you changed, or
does your city
not see the nights darkness,
anymore.

My Flower

15

I've danced
with thorns
I was told
to stay clear of.

It was
the flowers
that tore me
apart.

Cruel Universe

They speak,
that if you wholeheartedly
long for something,
the whole universe
will fight to
make it yours.

Even the universe
isn't on my side.
That's how wrong
you must be
for me.

Ungrateful

An emptiness,
something hollow,
a longing,
something missing.

I have everything,
except you.

Empty

I wish
the emotion you left,
had a voice.

It keeps growing
inside of me.
Although it is beautiful,
I can't breathe.

Timeless

I shall meet you again,
In another world,
in another life.

We shall be mere travellers,
crossing paths.
and I shall silently,
watch over you.

And finally
have the chance
to whisper
the sweetest of farewells,
one could ever,
receive.

Nostalgia

I look back
at the times
When I used to miss you,

Now that its ended
I miss those times
when I used to miss you.

The Next Chapter

I take the courage
to share my words
and show the world
my wounds
so that others
can heal.
Remember,
The story must go on.